I Need to Get Along with Different Types of People

Claudine G. Wirths
Mary Bowman-Kruhm

illustrated by
Laurie Spencer

J. WESTON

WALCH
PUBLISHER

Portland, Maine

Cover photo: ©1994 John Alphonse

1   2   3   4   5   6   7   8   9   10

ISBN 0-8251-2657-6

Contents

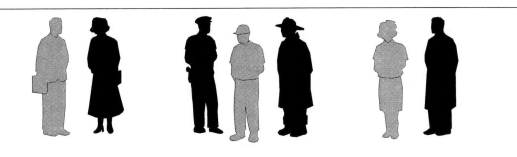

CHAPTER 1

How to Get Along—On the Job and Off

Which person do you think you most need to get along with on the job?

The boss, of course.

Nope. You. Yourself.

That's a good one. I get along with myself just fine.

Don't you ever get mad at yourself for doing something stupid? Or wonder why you worry about things when a worker near you doesn't seem to care at all? Or why someone who seems like an OK person won't take a coffee break with you?

> Well, yeah. Sure.

That's what we're talking about. If you want to get along, on or off your job, you need to find out why you're the way you are. You need to understand things like why you feel the way you do if the boss yells at you. Or why you hate to follow the rules for cleaning up your work site.

Getting along with yourself and feeling good about the way you are can also help you get along with others.

> On my job I pretty much do my own thing. It doesn't matter if I get along with others or not.

You may feel it doesn't matter, but bosses expect people to work together without a lot of problems. We think knowing about different types of people can help you get along with both yourself and others, including your boss.

> I don't think you can tell me anything to help me get along any better, not with some of the stuff going on at my job.

How about hearing us out before you decide? Lots of people—people like you—feel that learning about **type** helps them smooth out problems with others, both on the job and off. Here are the sorts of things they say:

- In my job I have to work with a lot of people, and knowing about type sure makes it easier to get along.

- Now I know why I hate office picnics and parties.

- I always wondered if I was the only one who felt that way about rules. Now I know I'm not.

■ Even my brother and I get along these days. I know why he acts the way he does sometimes—even if I think it's crazy.

■ I like myself a lot better now that I understand why I do some of the things I do.

This sounds pretty cool. Say more.

All right. Those who study this sort of thing think that each person in the world is one of four kinds. They believe that every individual has one of four basic patterns of behaviors, or types.

Stop right there. No way that every person is one of four kinds. There are hundreds of kinds of cars, so there must be a lot more kinds of people.

Four kinds of people will do it, if you look at the larger patterns. It's much like the cars you talked about. In spite of many makes of cars, all cars today work by only four ways: by gas power, by diesel fuel power, by electric power, or by you-push-it power (if you have an old clunker). People are powered too by one of four main ways, or types.

To help you remember each type and how a person of each type tends to act, we have given the types names. But remember, we made up these names only to help you keep them in mind. After all, a car called a Hornet doesn't sting or have wings. The person who names a car Hornet just wants you to remember it moves fast. Because we call one type *Actor*, for example, it doesn't mean the person is on TV. It just means that people who are Actors like to take action.

Here are the four types:

■ *Member.*   A Member likes to belong. Members plan ahead, play by the rules, and don't like change.

■ *Actor.*   An Actor loves action and change. Actors live for the here and now.

- *Thinker.*   A Thinker does a lot of thinking before doing anything. When Thinkers do act, they work hard at whatever they do.

- *Friend.*   A Friend tries to do what feels right inside. Friends think about the effect what they do will have on others.

Which is the best type to be?

None of the types can be said to be the best one. What matters is how people use their type, not the type itself. A person who is one type may do something to save a boss time and money. Someone else of the same type may do something to rip off the boss. There's no built-in good or bad for any type.

And you cannot look at only one thing someone says or does. Keep in mind the person's work *pattern.* Our pattern of thinking and acting starts in the early years and seems to last throughout life. You may think you know what type a person is, but the ways he or she acts over time will tell you if you are right.

That happened with a girl at work. She seemed to like me. Then at a party she hardly spoke. I sure changed my mind about her.

If we give you one more piece of the type puzzle, you may change your mind again. Here it is: Everyone is also either an *Inner* or *Outer.*

If being around other people usually makes you feel revved up, you are an Outer. If being around lots of people tires you out, you are an Inner.

Do you know someone who loves to go out to a big party to see old friends and meet new ones? If so, that person is no doubt an Outer. Outers not only love a party, they also hate it to end. They feel a real need to hook up with other people much of the time. They may hang out at the mall just on the chance of seeing someone they know.

Inners keep to themselves more. They may like a party, but it soon tires them out. They will be among the first—not the last, for sure—to leave when the party ends. Most of the time they choose to be alone or with only one or two close friends, working on a car, cooking, shooting hoops, playing cards, or whatever they like to do best.

I guess Friends are Outers.

No. Any type can be an Inner or an Outer. Many Friends are Outers, but a Friend can feel concern for others without hanging out with people all the time. In the same way, a person who is a Member, an Actor, or a Thinker can be either an Inner or Outer.

Sometimes I like to hang out at the mall, and sometimes I like to play video games by myself. Am I an Outer or an Inner?

We are talking about *most* of the time. Actually, each of us is partly an Outer and partly an Inner. But most of us are more often one way than the other.

In fact, being mostly one way or the other goes for everything we say about type. We may act like other types some of the time. But in a tight spot, we tend to be either an Inner or an Outer and to show our true type by acting the way that type does.

From what I've seen of my boss, I'd say he's the impossible type.

He may just seem that way because he is a very different type person from you. Now, if you can figure out what type your boss is and what type you are, you may be able to handle him a lot better.

There's no way I can handle this man. He's the kind who wants things done *his* way and *only* his way. Today he lined up the days we have to work this month. When we told him we didn't like it, he wouldn't let us switch. "No changes," he said. "This is the way it stays. If I start making changes, they'll never end."

So what are you going to do?

I guess I'm going to quit.

If we could tell you how you might be able to get the boss to change his mind, would you like to keep the job?

Sure. But there's no way he's going to change.

You are right, in one way. He seems to want you to follow his rules, and that won't change. But you may be able to get him to listen to what you have to say and change the work schedule. Once you understand type, you may be surprised what happens.

So how do I know which type I am and which type he is?

We'll look at the types one at a time. We'll talk about how the different types act and feel, what worries them, and what pleases them.

As we talk, think about which type is most like you. You may see a little bit of yourself in all of the types, but one is most likely to make you smile and say, "Yeah, that's me."

You said your boss didn't want to change the work schedule. That may be a clue that your boss is a *Member*. So, we'll first find out more about that type.

CHAPTER 2

Join the Club

All of us want to feel that we belong, that we are not alone. But *Members* feel a *need* to belong to some kind of group. They don't like change in their lives, and belonging to a group with rules and plans makes them feel secure.

> I guess everyone who plays on a basketball team must be a Member.

No, just because people are in a group does not mean they are Members.

So why aren't they, if Members are the kind of people who want to belong to a group?

People of every type belong to teams. But each person has his or her own reasons for wanting to join. Some want to join for the glory of winning or because they are good at the game. Others like to hang around with friends who are on the team. Someone else may be trying to get known in a new school. There are lots of reasons someone might want to play on a sports team.

Members may have some of those reasons too. But the big reason Members join a team is that being part of the team makes them feel good. Team sports have rules, and everyone has to follow the rules. Members like this feeling of knowing what to do and what is expected of them and everyone else.

Not everyone who is a Member likes sports. Some Members try to hang out with people who work in the same place or go to the same school or are in the same job-training program. Any of these groups can give them a feeling of belonging.

A Member is the kind of person who likes to say: "I'm a Bulls fan" or "I'm a Christian" or "I'm a Harley rider" or "I'm one of the Underpins Bowling bunch" or "I'm an Italian" or "I'm in the Garden Club." Members wear T-shirts or put stickers on their car to let other people know about their group.

What about gangs? Gangs are people who want to hang out together, so they must all be Members.

No. Same story as the basketball team. Young people who belong to gangs may seem as if they want to be together. Not all of them do. Just as people who are on a sports team have different reasons for playing ball, people who are in a gang join for different reasons. Some join because it seemed like fun at the time they were asked. Others join because they are afraid not to. Still others join because they don't want to make their brother or sister or best friend mad. You can, no doubt, think of other reasons.

But for sure, gangs are a type of group to which Members might be drawn, because most gangs have rules. The rules may not be written down, but they are known and followed by those in the group.

No matter what the group, some Members join it because they want to feel a bond—a sense of belonging—with other people in the group. They feel really sad (or maybe mad) if someone leaves the group, even if they don't like the person much. For them, change is a pain.

> What you've said so far sounds a lot like my boss. He belongs to a group that meets every Tuesday for lunch. He brags a lot about what they do to help the town.

You have hit on another reason Members join a group, besides liking to belong. They join because they have a strong sense of duty. Young people who are Members, for instance, often feel a very strong sense of duty to other members of their gang if trouble starts.

Adults, like your boss, may join a group like a civic club because they feel a sense of duty to the community where they live. They show their feelings when they say things like:

- We have to give back to this town some of what it's given us.

- Everyone should do something to help this city. It's their duty.

- This country has been good to me. I want to be good to it for the sake of my kids.

No matter what the group, Members feel a sense of duty toward what the group stands for. They feel that groups make their lives stable and solid.

> My uncle belongs to a group that meets every month, and they wear a special kind of shirt and hat when they meet. My aunt laughs at him, but my uncle gets really mad if his special shirt is in the laundry when he wants to wear it.

Your uncle is almost surely a Member. Even though other people may laugh at them for belonging to groups that wear strange hats or weird clothes, Members tend to be serious about that sort of thing. In high school many kids who are Members dress like a certain crowd, because that is part of playing by the unspoken rules.

Outer or Inner, one rule Members most often follow is being there right on time when the group gets together.

> I've heard my boss's wife say he's like that at home. He wants her to have his dinner ready at six every night. He even makes his kids take off their hats at the table. That's crazy.

Not to a Member. Members like to be on time, not only for work but also for events outside of work. And if the boss is a Member, he or she will no doubt make it clear that you are to be on time, look right, and put in a full workday.

> You've got it. A guy was late for work last week, and my boss wouldn't even listen to what he had to say. He said this guy has been late two times before, and a rule is a rule. He fired him.

Your co-worker learned two things the hard way about most bosses who are Members. (1) Being on time is very important. (2) Playing by the rules is important too.

Playing by the rules means Members who give their word stick by it—for better or for worse, as with your co-worker. But here's the plus side of playing by the rules: When your boss says you'll get a pay raise if you do a good job for the next three months, believe it. Do a great job, and he will give you that raise.

Here is one more plus that goes along with playing by the rules with Members: They are the up-front people that they seem to be. They seldom hide their cards under the table.

> I don't know about that. He sounds worried when he talks about the business, but he doesn't say what's going on.

We can't tell you how the business is doing, but we can say that worry is often part of the makeup of a Member, especially an Outer. They talk a lot of gloom and doom and fret about the worst that can happen. But they work hard not to let it happen.

Of course, in any business, things can go wrong that even bosses can't control. But bosses who are Members don't often make risky deals that may put you out of a job. Nor is a Member likely to ask you to take risks with your safety, over and above those that go with the job.

> What you say fits my boss. He also nags us a lot to keep our stuff in order: "Pick up" "Do this" "Watch out" is all we hear.

Members often nag a lot because it is their way of seeing that you follow the rules they think are important. On the other hand, we bet your boss does his own job well and doesn't expect more of you than he's willing to do himself.

> You've got that right. He does his own thing without a lot of blasting off about how good he is.

That too is like most Members. They do their work and don't say much. This is even truer for Inners than Outers. But both Inners and Outers are quick to jump on others who don't do a great job.

> Man, this Member sounds more and more like my boss.

Many bosses, male and female, are Members. Members like to supervise others to see that a job is done the way they think it should be done, so they like to be boss. Also, they stick to jobs long enough to work up to being the boss. Since they don't like a lot of change in their lives, they rarely are job-hoppers.

> Well, my boss is sure the don't-change-anything kind of person.

Because Members don't take chances, they believe in change only when they feel sure the changes will work for the better. They like to have the feeling that things won't change without good reason; and even then, they change slowly and with much thought.

That brings us to the problem you're having on the job. You said that you want your boss to try a new way of making out the work schedule. Now that you know what most Members are like, what do you think you can say so that your boss will at least listen to your ideas?

> Talking to my boss is hard. And he doesn't say things that make it any easier.

If your boss is an Inner, he wants to keep things to himself. He will tend to button up tight. Even Members who are Outers may seem cold when you talk to them. They will not try to put you at ease. But most Members are fair once you get their ear. So how could you go about it?

> I guess I should first ask if he'll talk to me.

Good start. You may want to ask for a meeting a few days from now. Members don't like to be caught off guard about anything.

> Should I say that some of the others are planning to quit too?

No, you should speak only for yourself.

And if any of them want to go with you to the meeting to speak for themselves, tell your boss ahead of time. Keep in mind that Members don't like surprises—and five workers when he thought he'd be meeting with only one would be quite a surprise.

Then, be on time for the meeting. And look clean and neat. Remember, Members like people who play by the rules. Get a good night's sleep so you have your wits about you. Now, what will you say?

> I guess if I say I'm mad and plan to quit unless he changes things, I'll just lose my job.

You' re right. Before you meet with him, think about things you can say, even if doing so is not easy for you.

Here are some ideas to keep in mind when you talk to a Member—whether boss, parent, or friend:

- Talk in a quiet voice. State the problem and why you are there. Members don't like shouting and name-calling (unless *they* are doing it).

- Give facts to back up what you say—just the facts, quickly and briefly stated.

- Talk about only the one problem. Don't get off the subject and list other things you'd like to change.

- Make sure what you say is useful and practical. Offer a good solution to the problem, one that leaves the boss in charge of things.

I guess I need to say how I'd like to change the work schedule.

You' re right. A good plan, thought about ahead of time, will help a lot. And remember, Members seldom care about high-flown ideas. Your boss will best like a plan that is practical, useful, and possible—one he knows other workers will buy into, especially one that will help the business in some way.

Good luck. Let us know how your talk goes.

CHAPTER 3

Do It Now!

Hello, again. We've been wondering if you met with your boss and suggested ideas for a new work plan. And if so, how did it go?

Yeah. We met two days ago. And it went pretty well. He isn't real happy, but he says he'll give my ideas a try, if the rest of the workers are willing to go by the new rules.

Good for you.

I felt as if I were being sort of sneaky to get my way.

Why did you feel sneaky?

That *type* stuff lets you get in someone's head and gives you one up on the other guy. But, I have to tell you, it made me feel good to change his mind—even if it wasn't fair.

We don't agree that using what you learn about the four types of people isn't fair. Let's say you have trouble knowing what to say to your boss when you bump into him at the watercooler. But you know he likes golf, so you ask him about his golf game. Would that be sneaky?

No, I think that would be pretty smart.

Using what you know about type to help you talk to people is the same. You used what you know about him and his type to make your point in a way that helped him understand you better. You didn't *make* him do anything.

Type helps you know how the other person thinks and what that person feels is important. Then you can work together better. Being able to work well with others—boss and co-workers—can mean success on the job. Not being able to work with someone can get you fired these days. More and more jobs require you to work closely with other people. Besides, if you are pleased with yourself and the way you get along with your boss and other workers, you will enjoy your job a lot more.

I'm glad I talked to my boss. But why did I still feel scared and nervous when he called me in to talk with him? I had planned what I was going to say.

You may have had trouble because *your* type may not feel at ease with *his* type. Also, your type may not often plan ahead of time what you will say, so you were not acting the way you usually do.

Knowing about his type helped you make your point. Knowing about your own type would help you be more at ease next time. Would you like to know what type we think you are?

> Hey, I'm one of a kind. I don't think I'm a type, no matter what you say about other people.

The way you say that makes us think that you are the type we call *Actor*. From some of the things you've said, we've been suspecting right along that you are an Actor. Even more than other types, Actors like to see themselves as one of a kind.

> But how can I be like others and still be one of a kind?

One Actor may own a fleet of airplanes but dress in sweatpants and sweaters. Another Actor may surprise folks when he jumps off his bike dressed in a suit and tie. Same type, but they show their one-of-a-kindness to the world in very different ways.

> Does anything else make you think I'm an Actor? No way will I ever go on TV.

You strike us as being a person who likes to be on the move. We call such people Actors because they are often active, not because they like to act on TV. They like doing things, moving around, and keeping busy. Actors who are Outers like to talk a lot and include other people in their actions. Actors who are Inners are happier doing things alone or with only one or two close friends. Inner or Outer, all Actors get bored easily.

Because they have to follow the rules and do the same thing every day, they often dislike school.

Because they like change in their lives, they often take jobs in which they have new things to do all the time. They are also very good at jobs in which they must think and act fast.

And because they can think and act fast, they often are the ones to get themselves and other people out of a mess.

I don't want to be a broom jockey.

We don't mean cleaning up a mess that way. We mean dealing with a problem. Let's say you and a co-worker work for a deli. You are trying to get trays of party food out of a van. Your co-worker dents the door of a new car parked next to you when he swings around with a big tray. The driver blows up and yells at your co-worker. The co-worker then gets really upset and doesn't know what to do.

You, being the Actor type, calmly talk to the car's owner. You tell him who owns the deli and what the owner's phone number is. You say how sorry everyone is, and you add other things to calm the person down. You step in to make the best of a bad scene. On the job or off, an Actor often excels at dealing with a problem quickly. For that reason, many Actors are good firefighters or rescue workers.

Maybe I *am* an Actor. One time I saw a car crash. A bunch of older people got out of their cars, but they just stood around. So I told everyone what to do. When the rescue squad got there, one guy thanked me for acting so fast.

Actors often are fast-acting. They live in the here and now. They don't stop to figure out why something is true, or trouble themselves with questions like "What might happen if…?" They do it now, whatever *it* is.

Acting fast can have a good side and a bad side. When you stepped in after the car was dented, you helped both your boss and co-worker by acting fast. But the co-worker who dented the car may have been an Actor too. He may have caused the problem by acting too fast. He wanted to get the job done and didn't stop to think of the trouble he could cause by grabbing a tray and jerking it out of the van without looking. Actors have to take care to think before they use their act-now side.

Well, what else is good about being an Actor? If I am one, I want to know that I'm cool.

Definitely cool. Actors love a good time and are fun to be with. This is more true of Outers than Inners, but even Inners tend to take life one day at a time and like to go where their mood takes them. Actors are the ones who jump up and say, "Let's call some friends over and order a pizza." A Member might stop, think, and say, "Well, I don't know. It's getting late and I have to get up early for work." But the Actor wants friends and food right then and would grab the phone.

> Actors are my kind of people.

OK, but don't forget Actors have problems. Actors often find daily or weekly tasks hard to carry out. Packing a lunch for work or making a bed or dumping trash every day is not something they like to do. Actors want to think they are free as birds, ready to fly high. Coming down to earth to grub for worms is not their thing. They often have to push themselves to do what others expect of them.

> You sound like my boss. When I told him my job was boring, he said I just had to put up with it until I work my way up to a job I like. He didn't seem to understand at all.

A Member wouldn't. Remember? They don't like change. Boring is often OK with them.

When Actors job-hunt, they need to keep in mind that some jobs are more boring than others. That's why, as boring as school or a training program may be, they can't afford to drop out. The less education or training people have, the more likely they are to end up in boring jobs for the rest of their lives. Since planning ahead is not an Actor's strong point, many Actors find it hard to do something just because there is a payoff down the road. That's one of the bad points about being an Actor.

> Maybe I'm not an Actor. I planned a big trip to the lake last year.

Remember what we said: Not everything about a type may fit everyone of that type in every way. Type means a basic pattern of how someone behaves, not how that person acts at *all* times. An

Actor-type boss, for instance, may curb his or her do-it-now style. After all, bosses can't just breeze off the job when the mood strikes—even if they would like to.

> **But what if I have a boss who's an Actor? What would I need to know?**

Here are some tips for you if you work with an Actor, whether boss or co-worker:

- Keep in mind that Actors generally enjoy taking risks. If you are an Actor also, working for one may be easier. We tend to feel more at ease with people who are the same type we are, often without knowing why. If you are not an Actor, realize that your boss may take risks that bother you. These risks can be big or small. Maybe the boss puts money into expanding the company at a time that seems unwise. Or the boss expects you to use equipment with no safety guard to cover a sharp edge. Not all Actors do those things, but be aware that type does matter in what one person worries about and another person doesn't.

- Remember, most Actors are great at bargaining. Since they deal well with people, you need to be ready for whatever they say. Asking for a pay raise or a day off? Have your reasons firmly in mind, and be ready to counter whatever your boss says. Actors love to win.

- Although an Actor may agree to do something, check to be sure that it gets done. You may even have to remind your boss. Actors don't mean to forget, but other things happen and they go with the flow.

- Stay ready for some great spur-of-the-moment office parties. Inner or Outer, Actor or not, drop your work and join in anyway. Actors don't like people who never relax and have fun. Work is not the most important thing in their lives.

Now that you know about the Actor type, what do you have to say?

I guess I'm an Actor, but I won't know for sure until I hear what the other types are.

Then let's look at the type we call the Thinker. You may have a co-worker now or a boss of that type some day.

No time to think about that now. But I promise to catch up with you soon.

It's a deal. We'll hold you to it.

CHAPTER 4

Think About It

Most people seem to be either Members or Actors. Not many people are the type we call *Thinker*. If you should have a Thinker for a boss, knowing what makes one tick could make life on the job a lot easier for you.

We said earlier that Thinkers do a lot of thinking about how to proceed before they act. Thinkers, both Inners and Outers, like to feel that they do well at whatever they try. Success means a lot to a Thinker.

Are Thinkers the brains who make all A's in school?

There are two answers to your question. First, Thinkers don't have to be brains. A person may not be at all smart and still want to try to understand something before doing it. Second, Thinkers tend to make A's in subjects they enjoy because they work so hard to succeed. If they like a class, they want to do the best job and earn the best grade they can. But getting a high grade just to get it doesn't mean that much to them. They get good grades because they work hard, and their grades tell them mainly that they have been successful.

But what if they don't like a class?

Then they may not try at all. They'll just do what they can to get by. Or they may even fail.

So a boss who's a Thinker would want workers in his company to do a good job.

Not just a good job. A great job.

If they're so set on doing a good—or great—job, does that mean work is their whole life?

For many Thinkers, the answer is yes. Their work is their life. Other Thinkers have a hobby instead, and they work at that hobby as if it were a full-time job. If they are Outers, the hobby will often include doing things with other people, but they want to be the ones who shoot the most baskets or own the most stamps or are the best shot in the club. Of course, an Inner prefers a hobby that allows for time alone or with only a few others. But Thinkers who pursue a hobby alone work just as hard to be successful at it.

Sounds like a Thinker-type boss could be hard to work for.

That depends on who *you* are. If you are a Thinker and value what you are doing and want to do a great job, you'd feel a boss of the same type is easy to work for. But if you are an Actor, you'd probably feel that working for that type of boss is hard.

What one person sees as a great boss, someone else sees as a terrible boss, based on *that person's own* type.

I'm not sure I see what you mean.

Here's another example: A boss who is a Thinker thinks long and hard about how to solve a job problem. This may be OK with workers who are Thinkers and Members. But an Actor may get mad at the boss. The Actor would have picked a way to go long ago, tried it out, and been well on the way to trying something else if the first way didn't work. The Actor can't see what the delay is.

From what a friend has told me, I have a hunch he may work with some people who are Thinkers. In fact, I bet his boss is a Thinker. Anything I can tell him that would help him work with her?

Thinkers will go along with change, even though they may take awhile to think the idea through. Outers are even more likely than Inners to have an eye out for a better way of doing something. Inner or Outer, many Thinkers are so open to making changes that they like to hear about new ideas.

Suppose your friend has the same kind of work-scheduling problem you had on your job. If he tells his boss he has an idea for a new way to draw up a work schedule that the other workers will like better, she will no doubt want to hear more. She may already have thought of other ways of her own to deal with it, but she'd like to hear his too.

That sounds great. I had to talk a lot to convince my boss even to hear me out.

On the other hand, a Thinker often doesn't wait to hear that there is a problem. As boss, the Thinker may upset workers who are Members by making changes just for the sake of change. Of course, this is one time when an Actor often gets along well with the boss.

My friend says his boss is good at getting everyone to pull together on a job. Is that true of Thinkers?

Yes, Thinkers seem born to lead. They pride themselves on being able to "see the big picture."

The flip side of this trait is that while they focus on the big view, they get restless with the little stuff. So they often come up with ways that seem a little off-base to other types. Let's say a Member, a Thinker, and an Actor mow lawns. The Member, no doubt, picks one way to cut grass and uses the same plan every time. The Actor rushes through mowing the lawn one time, and then talks someone else into swapping for a different job, maybe gassing up the mowers or doing the trim work. The Thinker, on the other hand, tries lots of ways to mow the lawn. The Thinker mows back and forth, in a circle leading in, in a circle leading out, and so on—ways that don't seem to make sense to the other two types. The Thinker is looking for the best way to do the job, but is also trying to break up the boredom of doing the same thing again and again.

That makes me think of something else my friend told me. He said his boss sometimes doesn't follow through. She promised the workers some new lockers, but she never bought them.

This trait of Thinkers goes hand in hand with being bored with routine chores. Bosses who are this type leave the details for others to take care of. They are quite happy to have others, usually Members, carry out the little tasks that keep the office or work site running day to day.

Think about what your friend's boss has to take care of before she can buy the lockers. She has to check where lockers are sold for the best price. Then she has to write a memo telling the workers about the plan to install the lockers, plus carry out the nitty-gritty to make the plan work. If your friend knew that his boss was a Thinker and knew all the details involved, he might not have been surprised that the lockers never arrived.

So they'll never get any new lockers?

Just as knowing something about your boss helped you talk with him, knowing how a Thinker acts can help your friend with his boss. Your friend could wait for weeks for the boss to check out the prices. During that time, he and the others would grouse and grumble about the boss behind her back. They might even get angry that the plan seemed to have been stopped or dropped.

Or, knowing that Thinkers hate detail work, your friend could suggest that he check out two or three supply stores for the best prices on lockers and installation charges. The plan would start rolling as soon as he got back to the boss with the prices. Your friend, the boss, and the company would all be further ahead that way.

> One other thing bothers my friend about his boss. His boss sometimes makes nasty comments about a person's work. She says things that hurt people, right in front of the whole crew.

Many Thinkers, including bosses, make sharp comments. Although they don't set out deliberately to hurt someone, they seldom care who hears them. They want a job to be well done, and they say sharp things if that doesn't happen. Since Thinkers pride themselves on fairness, most of their remarks are usually true, even if they hurt. So smart workers listen to what is behind the mean remark and clean up their act.

Inner or Outer, Thinkers tell the truth, but tend to tell it in a way that is often biting and hurtful. To be fair, they are as hard on themselves as on others.

Most of the time, however, Thinkers are in a good humor. Outers seem to love a good laugh and do it easily. We must admit though, Outers tend to brag about themselves more than most people of other types do.

> But my friend says his boss seldom says thanks or notices when someone has done a good job.

That too is a trait of Thinkers. If they do praise someone, once is enough. If your friend were to ask his boss how she feels about his work, she might say, "I'm surprised you asked. I remember telling you last year that you're doing well." Thinkers feel that if they say it once, no matter how long ago, they don't need to say it again.

In short, Thinkers expect a job to be well done, whether they do it or someone else does it. Gushing with praise is not their thing.

Wow. I'm not sure I can keep all this in my mind to tell my friend.

Here are the basic facts to pass on to him. To work for a Thinker, no matter what type you are:

- Expect your boss to hate mistakes. Thinkers want not just good but *great* jobs done by themselves and those who work for them.

- Don't expect your boss to handle details. The most you can hope for is that the boss will pick someone to take care of detail work.

- Don't be surprised by what your boss says or does. A Thinker may be gifted in a field you never dreamed of and not have shown it before. This is often true of Inners, who keep secret talents to themselves.

- Let the boss do much of the talking. Thinkers who are Outers may take over when you talk, and may brag and joke.

- Don't expect your boss to say something more than once. Praise, ways to handle a task, anger that a job wasn't done well—Thinkers seldom repeat themselves.

- Shrug off sharp things the boss says, no matter how cutting, as just being the way a Thinker is. That *is* the way one is.

OK. I'll try to remember all that to tell my friend. Is that it on this *type* stuff?

Not quite. There is one more type. We call this type *Friend*, but it doesn't mean just what you mean by the word *friend*. Next, we'll fill you in on the Friend type.

CHAPTER 5

A Friend Is a Friend—
Most of the Time

There is one more type you need to know about, if you want to be able to get along with almost everyone. As we said, most of the people in the world seem to belong to the two big groups we call Members and Actors. Fewer by far are in the group of Thinkers we just met. About the same small number are in the last type group we'll talk about—the type we call *Friend*. What matters most in life to them are other people.

> Hey, that's me. I thought I was an Actor. I spend more time with my friends than I do with my family. And my friends are the ones who know me best.

Clearly, your friends are extra special to you. But that doesn't mean you are mostly a Friend type. You may or may not be. There's a lot more to being a Friend than just getting along with people.

Like what?

Friends truly feel that other people give meaning to their lives—people whom others might call strangers, as well as people who are close to them. Before doing anything, Friends often think about how what they say and do will affect someone else.

I guess I'm not that type. I don't spend my life worrying about other people.

Friends do. What makes Friends different is that they think about most things *from the point of view of other people*. For example, Friends may:

- hear a story on TV about a disaster on the other side of the world. They feel pain for the people who have been hurt and send money to the Red Cross.

- see a person who has had too much to drink and worry about how that person will get safely home. They may offer a ride.

- spend a long time listening to the problems of someone else. No matter if they just met the person, they still want to listen.

Friends sound as if they go through life being do-gooders.

Some of them are do-gooders. Some of their type are also "do-badders." They may take advantage of being able to make others feel special. A Friend, for instance, might sweet-talk his aunt into lending him money for a car. Even if the aunt needs the money herself, she will end up feeling glad she gave it to him.

Most of the time, though, Friends choose to help others.

Do they look for jobs that let them be helpful?

Yes, they often have jobs in which they help others. They find working for and with others personally rewarding. The jobs they like cover a wide range: being in the clergy, teaching, handling returns at a store, and admitting patients for a doctor are just a few of them.

But in any job, or even away from work, Friends truly focus on the person they are with and make the person feel special. Many times they can sense how a person feels before the person does! Friends also have a way of listening that can make things seem better to the person talking, even if the Friend has said or done very little.

On the other hand, taking on the problems of others is one way that Friends can get into trouble. Too much worry about what someone else should do or about what happened to another person can take a big toll. A Friend may have a real problem on the job if thinking and fretting and talking about someone else's problems cuts into work time.

What if the boss is a Friend?

On the job, of course, a boss who is a Friend often listens carefully to every worker. That's true whether the worker's problem is one on the job or one brought to work from the outside.

If your boss is a Friend, you will no doubt also have chances to grow on the job. Friends tend to accept people as they are, but also do their best to help them change and grow. Their satisfaction comes from helping others change. On the job, they may set aside time for training. They may call meetings to be sure all the workers know what to do. They may assign all new workers to a partner who can help them and give them support.

Friends want those who work under them to do a good job, and they also want them to be happy with themselves and their work. Friends usually draw out the best in others.

Will a boss who's a Friend tell me how I'm doing on the job?

Bosses of other types may say little about your work. They may tell you, "Great job," or, "You were late today. Be on time Monday." They may say almost the same thing to everyone who works for them. But a boss who is a Friend will tell you special things, usually good things, even stretch the truth a little. Then, the Friend will point out things you can do better. What the boss says will be remarks that apply only to you.

Sounds as if a Friend is a great person to work for.

Like all types, a Friend can be. Also like all types, a boss who is a Friend can be a problem—especially for other types. Friends are willing to hear what someone has to say and talk about ways to deal with what is wrong. But, sad to say, they don't like to deal with problems that involve their doing something that might make someone else dislike them.

This means that, as boss, a Friend may not face up to someone other workers see as big trouble. The Friend hopes that by doing nothing, the problem will go away. But problems generally do not go away.

Friends are also stressed out by fighting. They get upset with people who argue and whine and nag, and they tend not to want such people around—even though the people are good workers and may be bringing up problems that need to be handled. Friends get so upset by the fighting and nagging that they miss the problem or choose not to face it.

So keep it cool on the job....

Right. No matter what type you are, to work with a boss who is a Friend, you should try to do the following:

- Avoid fights with words or action. Friends hate arguing and fighting and whining of any type; they want people to get along with others on the job.

- Try not to sound as if you blame the boss, even when you have to talk about something you feel should be changed. Use words that don't fault the Friend when you state the problem. Say, "Can you help me find out why my check didn't come?" Don't say, "You forgot to mail my check." Asking Friends for help takes advantage of their basic wish to reach out and be liked.

■ Don't think, because your boss listens to what you have to say, that he or she will always act on your ideas or advice. Friends, especially Inners, listen because they care about you and what you feel and say, but they may not tell you when they don't agree.

■ Expect very personal praise and comments about how you do on the job.

■ Ask your boss to say things another way if you don't know what he or she means. Friends tend to speak in broad and general ways. No "Here's how to do it—Step 1, 2, 3" for them. If what they say is not clear to you, check it out with them. Don't go away confused and shaking your head. If the boss says, "Spend more time on the paint problem," ask, "Are you saying you want me to find out how much the paint costs and tell you, or do you want me to buy some paint and start painting?"

■ If you have a real problem, expect the boss to help you. The Friend really does care about you—up to a point. While you have the problem, the boss will spend lots of time with you. But once the problem is solved, the boss won't have as much time for you anymore. Bosses who are Friends often spend too much time with the problem workers and not enough time with the workers who are getting along OK.

I think I'd get along pretty well with a Friend for a boss.

You said you thought you might be an Actor, and Actors usually get along pretty well with Friends. There is a lot of Actor in most Friends. But suppose you were a different type. Let's look more closely at how different types get along with each other and work together.

CHAPTER 6

Types You'll Meet on the Job

One of the greatest things about understanding type is that you learn you're not a bad person. You have strong points. You have weak points. The same goes for other people. Other people are not basically bad either.

When you become aware of how type works, the ways other people act make more sense. Sure, just like you, others can use their strong or weak points to do good things or bad things. But most of the time we all just cruise along and tackle life the way our type does. What other people call "bad" about you is probably nothing more than not being their type. And the same thing goes for people who bother you. You just have to plan around your type or the other person's type if you want to get along.

I'm not sure what you mean.

Suppose you are an Actor, the kind of person who doesn't have a built-in clock to get you to places on time. You don't go out of your way to make people mad because you are late, you just don't think about time. If you are meeting a friend who is a Member, you know time matters to that person. So buy yourself a cheap watch with an alarm—and set it to remind you to leave home on time. You understand why you can present a problem for the other person, and you do something about it.

But suppose I am a Member waiting for the other person who is always late?

You could do a couple of things. You could specify a meeting time a half hour earlier than necessary, or you could take along a paperback book to read while you wait, so you won't be steamed up when the other person arrives at last. Many Members have learned to carry work to do while waiting for other people.

Knowing about type can give you some ways besides fighting to handle real trouble.

Hey. Are you saying I should just give in to someone who's giving me trouble? Even if I'm not the one who started it?

No, that's not what we are saying at all. Let's look at an example: Suppose the guy who works next to you is always talking. He can't stick to his job for five minutes without telling you about his problems.

If I'm an Actor too, I'd get along with him, wouldn't I?

You would understand him, but you might not like him. People who are the same type tend to see things from the same point of view and have the same basic ways of acting. But they may show the world their behaviors in very different ways.

In this case, let's talk about the way you each show your type: He is an Outer and he likes to talk all the time about what's going on in his life; you like to finish your work in a hurry so you can get extra time for a coffee break. When he talks to you, you are slowed down because you can't keep your mind on what you need to do.

One week his car's starter switch breaks, and he spends a lot of time telling you how down that makes him feel. The next week his girlfriend breaks up with him, and he lets you know how sad he is. A few days later he makes up with her, and he can't stop telling you he is on top of the world. Then a friend is involved in a wreck, and he spends all his time talking about his friend's problem. And so on. He's a nice guy, but a crisis is always happening in his life—and he has to talk about it. And talk about it. And talk about it. And talk about it.

> Man, a guy like that would drive me crazy. After a while I'd slug him.

Do you think starting a fight would help?

> It might shut him up for a while.

Maybe for a very little while. Or it might make him mad at you, and he would cause you trouble in another way—trouble that might get one or both of you fired. But in the long run, it would not change his talking all the time. What else could you do?

> I guess I could go to the boss and ask to move my work site away from the guy. Or I could ask the boss if I could play a radio at work. Maybe I could bring in earphones and stick my own radio in my pocket. Or I could tell the guy about another job he might like better.

In a few seconds, you thought of lots of great ways around the problem—ways that could work since both of you are Actors. Once you accepted that the basic way the fellow acts is not likely to change, you began to think of ways you could do something about him—instead of getting into a fight.

If I can change the way I act, why can't he change the way he acts?

You are not really changing the way you act. You are not likely to change the basic way you act, any more than the other person is. What you do is think about your own type, and about his type, and pick a way to change the work setting that will let you get on with your job.

What if the co-worker isn't an Actor? Suppose he is a Member?

Going from crisis to crisis is not likely for a Member. If a Member has any crisis in life, it is probably not of his or her own doing. Members don't like too much change in their life. They prefer life to glide smoothly along.

But couldn't a Member who's an Outer have the problem of talking a lot?

For sure. And if you thought he were a Member, you would choose a different way to deal with the problem. Think back to what we said about talking to your boss, who is a Member. Many of the same things would be true. Members—bosses and workers—tend to like to talk problems through without a lot of yelling and fighting. They also seem to hear facts more than they sense feelings, and they want to be seen as doing their job. At the first coffee break, you could tell your co-worker that the talking keeps you from getting your job done. You might add that if the boss heard him talking so much, the boss no doubt would think he isn't getting *his* work done either. You could add that, if he looks around, he will see that no one else talks as much as he does. And even though there is no rule against talking, working quietly seems to be the unspoken rule.

What if he is a Thinker?

If he is a Thinker, you could call on his sense of wanting to do a job well also. You might say you are worried that he will get fired if the boss sees him talking so much. Being fired would make a Thinker feel he had failed, a feeling he surely does not want. You might suggest a time when you would be glad to hear him out, like lunch that week or dinner at a fast-food place on Monday after work.

What do you think you would say to him if he were a Friend?

I guess I'd say people, especially me, don't like so much talking.

Right, but you would say it very gently. Use some of your Actor charm in talking with him. Say some good things first. Perhaps you could tell him that he has always been fair with you, or that he has helped you out a couple of times. In other words, make him see that you like a lot of things about him. Then go on to say that you need his help. You are glad he likes you enough to talk to you, but when you listen to him you don't get your job done and you really need the coffee break every day.

I still want to know why I should be the one to think about other people's type. They ought to be thinking about mine.

You're right. That is one reason a lot of bosses now teach all workers about type. They find that the more people understand each other, the better everyone gets along.

Even if your boss doesn't train everyone about type, you still come out ahead by what you know. If you deal with people as if they are OK and you understand why they may act very differently from you, you have a lot more control over what happens to you. You can hope they will think about your type. In the meantime, try to avoid doing things that make you feel ill at ease. Find ways to do things that make you feel good. That's important, no matter what other people do or don't do.

It's your life. Enjoy it!

CHAPTER 7

Just Your Type of Job

One way to make the most of your type is to have a job that seems right for your type. By matching your type and your job, you are more likely to be happy and get good job reports.

> I'm happy with my job now, but sooner or later I think I'll want to move on. Any tips?

As you job-hunt, keep in mind two questions:

- How does this job match my being an Inner or Outer?

- Does this job suit someone of my type?

What if you are very much an Inner? No matter how good a job as a waiter or a store clerk sounds, it may not be for you. Both of these jobs would force you—every day, all day—to talk to lots of people you have never met. Keeping a smile on your face and doing great work would be hard for you. Look for a job that lets you work alone or talk with only one or two people during the day.

On the other hand, if you are an Outer, jobs such as waiter and clerk could be at the top of your list. Outers need jobs that let them talk with other people during the day.

In the long run, most of us are happier with jobs that let us be our deep-seated Inner or Outer self and our own natural type—jobs that let us act the way we feel most at ease. So don't pick a job just because it is close to home, the money is good, a teacher or parent recommends it, or other such reasons.

So what job would suit my type?

We can't tell you by name just what job you should have. But here are things each type should keep in mind when job-hunting:

Member

- Look for a job that has clear guidelines for you to follow.

- Look for a job that you can stay with a long time. Most Members prefer not to job-hop.

Actor

- Try to find a job that truly interests you so you are not tempted to job-hop.

- Inner or Outer, active jobs are better than jobs that force you to stay in one place.

■ Don't take a job that has lots of rules to follow, or one that forces you to do the same thing in the same way, day in and day out.

Thinker

■ Look for a job that offers you a chance to do some thinking for yourself.

■ Pick a job you can "buy into," one you will really like to do.

■ If the grind of doing the same thing every day bores you, look for a job that presents you with lots of new things to do.

■ Especially if an Outer, think about your hobbies. You may be able to turn a hobby into a job.

Friend

■ Try to find a job that builds on your feelings as a people person, your wanting to help others.

■ If an Inner, look for a job in a small office or job site.

As hard as work is to find, if I lose my present job, I may have to take almost anything offered. I may not be able to worry about what type I am and what type I should be to do the job.

True, good jobs are hard to find. Sometimes you have to take whatever you can get just to make some money. But in your off-hours, keep on job-hunting for the right job, or you may find yourself either jumping from one bad job to another, or stuck doing work you hate. When you job-hunt, you really can't afford *not* to think about your type. Why? Because you'll put in about fourteen thousand working days before you retire someday.

You've convinced me. But how would I convince someone to give me a job that is just right for me?

Type can help you when you interview. A résumé is a good thing for all types to have in hand, particularly because many bosses are Members, who value such things. The time it takes to write, type, and copy a résumé can pay off. But the résumé has to look great and say things that will sell you. Don't panic if you don't have one. You can pay to have someone write and type one for you. Or, better yet, trade leaf-raking or housecleaning or other work to someone who will help you with a résumé.

But a résumé alone won't get you the job that's right for you. Everyone also needs to keep in mind certain things about their type when they talk to a boss or an interviewer. Here are some special things for each type to think about before and during an interview.

Member

- If you are an Inner, role-play job interviews with a teacher, parent, or friend before you start looking for work.

- Don't be shy about selling yourself, especially if you are an Inner. A job interview is the place to talk about your skills.

- Ask if you will be trained or, at least, if a co-worker will be appointed to show you how to do the job.

- Be sure you are clear about what the company wants you to do.

- Ask about the chances of moving up on the job.

- Notice whether people who work there seem to get along and cooperate with each other. Outers need to check on this more than Inners do.

- Try not to feel let down if you aren't hired right away. Keep telling yourself that you *will* get a job that's right for you.

Actor

- Plan what you will say in an interview, even if your type doesn't like to do this sort of thing. You might forget to say some important thing if you just speak without rehearsing.

- Remember to dress in about the same way as those people who do the job you want. How you look is important.

- An interview is no time to play down what you can do, but don't try to con the person you're talking to. Don't say you can do all kinds of things you've never done before and have no idea how to do. For example, if writing is hard for you, don't lead the boss to think you'll take care of written reports.

- Check to see whether the job has lots of rules that you will find hard to follow, or tasks that will soon bore you.

- If you have done a lot of job-hopping, admit it. Then be ready to explain why.

- If you have hopped from one job to the next lots of times, ask for at least one day to think about taking the job, if it is offered to you. Think hard about why you have left so many jobs. Talk to people who know you. Ask yourself, "Is this job so much like my others that I'll soon quit?" If the answer is yes, keep looking.

Thinker

- Find out as much as you can about the job ahead of time so that if they offer you the position and tell you to take it or leave it, you'll have had time to think about it already.

- Don't forget to take a shower and dress neatly.

- Plan some friendly things to say at the start of the interview, especially if you are an Inner.

- Don't say "clever" things critical of your last job, boss, or co-workers.

- Check to see whether the job has rules that you will find hard to follow.

Friend

- List your skills ahead of time in your mind and on paper. Better yet, prepare a job résumé.

- Be your friendly self, but keep in mind that being friendly is not enough. A boss wants someone who has the skills to do the work.

- Even if the job sounds great, check into just what the company wants you to do. You don't want to be unhappy later when you find out the small details of your work load.

- Check to see whether people on the job site seem to get along with each other, and if this seems like an upbeat place to work.

- If an Outer, answer all questions, but resist the urge to talk on and on. Don't say that you can do things you really can't do, or that you are interested in a job that really isn't the best use of your skills.

- If you are turned down for a job, know that it is not the end of the world. Call another Friend and talk about it.

Is there anything else I need to know about type on the job?

Type helps you know your strong points. Focus on those strong points in doing your work and in getting along with your boss and co-workers. By thinking about type, you can avoid doing things that annoy your boss (especially when you don't mean to). You will be able to get along better with the other people on the job; that means a lot more fun for everyone as well as more work done well. Overall, you can look forward to enjoying yourself and your job. With a little luck, that may even mean a bigger pay check before too long. We hope you get it. You're the right type.